The World Eats Love

Carol Edwards

The World Eats Love

Copyright © 2023 Carol Edwards
First published in Australia in April 2023 by The Ravens Quoth Press

All characters and events in this publication, other than those clearly in the public domain, are fictitious and any resemblance to real persons, living or dead, is purely coincidental.

All rights reserved. No part of this production may be reproduced, stored in a retrieval system, or transmitted, in any form or by any means, electronic, mechanical, photocopying, recording or otherwise, without the prior permission of the publisher and copyright owner.
ISBN:
ISBN:

Cover design by Dawn Burdett
Formatting by Kara Hawkers
Editing by Kara Hawkers and E. Mery Blake

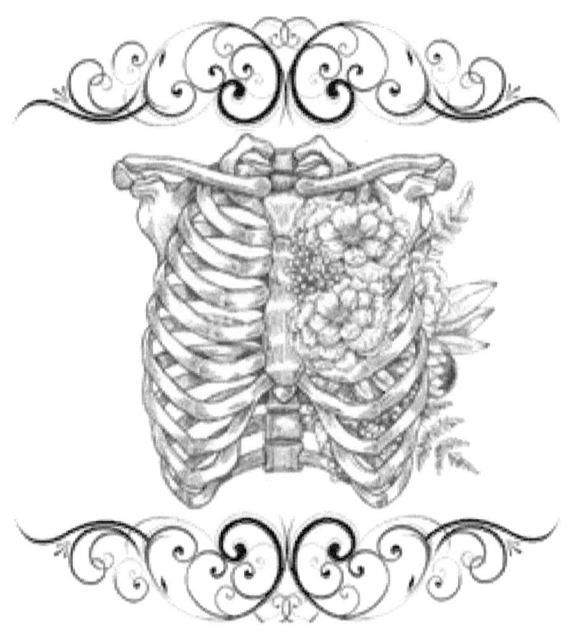

for the luminous Lisa Walsh, poetic kindred spirit
and
for Ashlee Shepherd, sweet friend too soon gone.

Contents

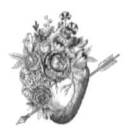

PEELING A TANGELO 17

UNDEAD 21

OUR HUNGERS 22

TATTOO 23

HURLED WISHES 25

LAST. WORDS 27

SACRIFICE 29

OLD SWEATSHIRT 30

DAYDREAMS 32

INSTRUCTIONS TO BREAK YOUR OWN HEART 34

WHAT REMAINS: 37

HAUNTED 39

SPECTRUM IN BLUES 41

"FROM MOONSTONE CRUSHED" 44

CAROUSEL HORSE 45

DEPTH 46

AUTUMN RUINS 48

LAST. TIME 50

REUNION 52

TRAINS 54

IN MEMORY 56

FORGOTTEN DREAMS 58

GROW UP 59

GROOMED 63

MOUNTAIN 66

HER VERSION ISN'T YOU 67

DARKENED STAGE 68

BIRD OF PREY 69

WHEN THE MONSTER UNDER YOUR BED HAS BECOME YOUR FRIEND 71

TO MY SWEET FLOWER 74

PETALS...76

THE LOVE VINE..78

HISTORY...80

DID IT HURT WHEN YOU FELL? 81

SOMETHING SWEET..................................83

MY LOVE...84

LAST. STEP..85

THINGS ARE LOUDER WHEN IT'S COLD..87

THE FALL...88

AVALANCHE..90

NORMALIZE 91

LAST. BREATH 92

I'M THE LUNGS NOW 94

APPARITION 96

FORBIDDEN 98

SHALLOW GRAVE 101

DEEP WATER 102

SHELL LINING 104

MIDNIGHT OASIS 106

WAITING 107

MOTHS 111

SNOWBOUND 112

WINDOWS 113

STAR-SONG... 115

WHISPER-STEPS OF THE REALLY-REAL ... 116

ACROSS DARK WATERS 118

FOUND 119

THE LONELY SHOES: A SHORT STORY .. 123

ACKNOWLEDGEMENTS 133

ABOUT THE AUTHOR.............................. 137

ABOUT THE PUBLISHER 141

Carol Edwards

Peeling a Tangelo

How strange a thing it is

to stop short in the kitchen

mid-peel over the trash

and marvel at the translucence

of a tangelo slice

sunlight plumped inside

a thin skin so easily burst,

shadow of the pit

a bit forward in its demand

to be granted analogy.

Perhaps it is the second or third

meaning in a poem,

mysterious and indistinct

but clearly visible

when one holds the verses

up to the light like a color slide,

though application of force

to squeeze it out mars form and feeling

and makes a gushy mess.

Maybe let the seed be

and eat it with the rest—it may

gestate inside a while

become nothing, just break down

and expel, or perhaps it will stick around,

settle into your cells,

which is what it intended anyway.

The World Eats Love

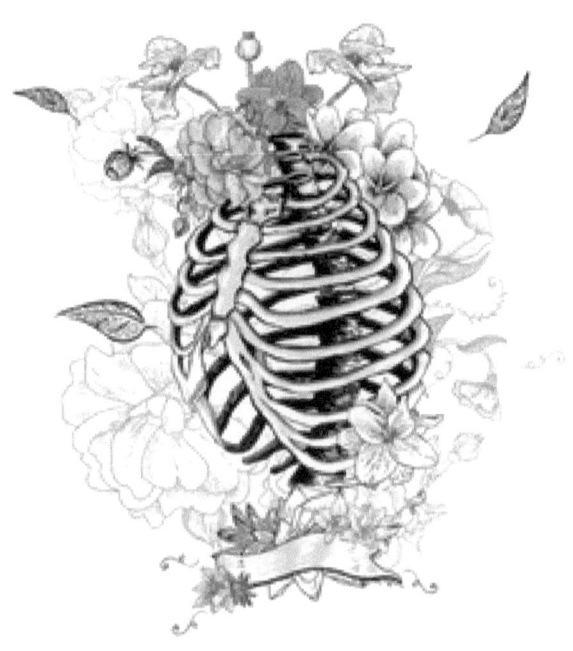

Carol Edwards

Undead

dreams…
    hopes…
        home…

these words resurge a lot—

    my hands return empty
    grasping for different ones—

their ghosts cling

    like corpses carried
    from grave to grave
    unwilling to abandon
    what might live again

Love

the only thing,   I realized
that walks on its own
emaciated to skin and bones

    immortally stitching stolen limbs
        organs

ceaseless hunger pangs
haunted
by things broken
    lost

Carol Edwards

Our Hungers

all within us hide, sedated lightning's

icy burn quietly caged

rumbles and scrapes

a tamed dream rage, soon lulled

back to sleep, leaking tempests

through our eyes

until one too many breaks—

trusts, hopes, hearts, bones—

cracks the haze muting their claws,

then like a dragon wakes, screams

un-numbed, and we gut

ourselves from inside trying

to contain the beast

who starves like we for warmth, rest,

peace

suffering abate,

dying a little each day

the will to fight slowly chipped away.

Tattoo

Prints trip down my inner arm

drip down

Through my fingertips

Driplets, drops

red memories

Tiny dots of light

trail after me

Constellations

In a crushing vacuum

squeeze air out my lungs

Carol Edwards

oceans leak past

lacrimal dams, avalanches

crash at concave glass

spill out spillways, flooding planes

other hand clutches

at the long line gash

running upstream, rushing

raw and rasping along my veins

Light stabs in prism shards

Rainbows tainted gray

Out, damned spot splotch stain

Crimson clover puddled gore

pooled on the tile floor

My insides melted down, smelted

sunshine hopes dissolved

into bone dust pressed on my scarred face

unseeing eyes trace the ghosts haunting us.

Hurled Wishes

I don't sleep in my bed anymore.

It's too full of dark thoughts, memories;

they clump together, lumps

pushing into thin skin—

bad dreams, angers, griefs

that nightly summon me to lay offering

on this altar of brokenhearted bitterness

knotted sheets my high priestess robes

sweltering, suffocating, drawing out

incensed ravings

swelling in my skull;

their rites demand the slaying

of my energy, my rest

bloodletting creativity and joy—

gods bent on swallowing

their vassals whole.

Carol Edwards

Now I lay me down to sleep

on the hard floor, locked door to keep

the mad frenzy out; this room

has no such memories, fresh as earth

waiting to enfold tenderly

fragile seeds—

with it I would cover me

beg sanctuary in its temple

where green innocent things

silently root,

unfurl delicate leaves

like the wishes I've hurled up to shooting stars

that only plummet back down

and some poor soul

mistakes them for magical things,

whispers their deepest needs,

hope for relief big enough to choke on.

Last. Words

I wasn't thinking about you when I died.

I was thinking about me

about the unbearable cruelty

of having to stay trapped here

in the cage I shaped for myself

not knowing what my hands made

until too late, put myself in

never to escape.

I wasn't thinking about you, how the news

might sucker punch you in your gut,

how you might feel cold, empty,

guilty you hadn't seen the signs

then burning rage at how dare I

declare I love you and leave you behind,

the pieces of yourself you gave

with me in a grave.

Carol Edwards

I wasn't thinking about you waiting for me

so many years

to realize what to me felt airtight

you could break from outside,

and you doubting why I never asked—

until now, I didn't know I could.

Sacrifice

Not all like phoenixes rise

from ash remains wreathed in flames:

as Sisyphus cursed to roll a boulder

ever uphill

some die daily quiet deaths

no voices to sing laments

lay us down in a shrouded grave

fertile with tears

to rise next morn

a seed through stone sprouting

ever seeking sun's light

though it shrivel and scorch

faithful to the Love we bear

clipped wings crying to feel the air.

Carol Edwards

Old Sweatshirt

You pretend its arms are my arms

Wrapped around your waist

My chest to your back

Keeping you warm on cold days

The red thread from my heart knit

Into something you hide yourself in,

Tuck your knees up underneath

And your hands in the sleeves

Until nothing but your toes

Peek out, maybe your nose

Nestled in the collar that smells of my cologne.

The tag brushing your neck is my breath

A ghost all that's left

From what short time I called you mine

Lips to your hair pressed,

The memory as fleeting as a breeze

To desert heat brings relief

Or rain to parched ground where seeds sleep

Comatose til by its kiss awaked

Sleeping princess cursed

To push through stone and ash

Rebuild the ruins fire left in her path.

Carol Edwards

Daydreams

hazy veils draped over the razor edge

graphics of "real," clean lines blurred

to watercolor, whole scenes

and lives and worlds layered over

the mundane, like songs

in the back of my brain filling the gaps

in day-to-day,

muting jagged ends, feeding

what I'm missing, missing out on,

fuel for anxiety in pain, salve for loneliness

that makes it so much worse

when the lie turns off;

stores every book I ever read,

the self-insert narratives I craft into them,

broken records played after played after played

until the crackled warping

tune disintegrates;

where I keep the futures and presents

I wish I'd had, bittersweet

visions that first ring heavenly

then slowly melt to a Munch-Dalí dressed hell,

demons therein of my own make,

fallen angels who follow me

hungry for the Dark I carry,

what wants all things like itself to break,

that stains my window eyes black

to keep out the Light I'd die to get back.

Carol Edwards

Instructions to Break Your Own Heart

First,

You must learn to emotionally attach—

pets, plants, a pair of pants, a pullover from a friend

whose name you'd never forget

because of how they made you feel.

Second,

Find a person who treats you the same—

appreciated, accepted, approved

with little hints of affection

secrets between you two

and tie your happiness to them. A text gives you

that split-second heart hitch;

a call, delight. The kind of greedy

where messaging them ten times a day

seems too little

you have so much you want to say.

Share at least all your life with them:

hobbies, humor, selfies

dreams. Unearth nicknames;

keep your phone close

to play "no you first"

at 2 a.m. when you need sleep.

Third,

Tell yourself everything is fine

when the texts slow. When they tease that

they only listen to half of what you say.

When your excitement hits your side of the screen

and drops, like prayers on the ceiling.

When your visits start getting cumbersome,

and they gripe to have to drive "so far."

When they reply two words.

When gifts are burdens

and silence reprieve.

Fourth,

Listen to the critic in your head when it says,

"You're too much."

"It was a joke."

"You're annoying."

"They're avoiding you."

"They don't care anymore."

Fifth,

Truth or lies, the words chip, chip

with hammer and chisel til your heart cracks

and tears run worn tracks

and breaths sing haunting songs

over hollow rib spaces,

scattering powdered ruby bits

fine as sand, the larger slabs

barely hanging from cirrus thin threads:

an anamorphic marionette.

What Remains:

the hole you opened when you left

    ribs encasing a cold cavity

          drowned

        in nothingness

      unable to draw full breath;

the scent

      of your skin

   anti-perspirant   cologne

      saturated in my clothes

   I will never wash them again;

places where you used to sit

lightly tinged   with bitterness

   like burnt coffee

        or tinnitus

     where once I heard the Song;

wan irises leaking saline

    to feed

        the macabre melancholies

    that refuse obsequies;

guilt

    for loving anything so much

        for being good

    but not enough

a glass and brass gilded crown.

Haunted

Voices linger in this house,

cracks and corners breathe in echoes,

carpets stained with memories.

Sitting on the floor,

sunlight creeps shadow leaves

across my knees, up the wall

until they blend in dusky hue

with the gray residue of loss, grief

dyes of pain soaked in curtains,

painted on door frames.

Laughter may be somewhere still,

but I find it so light it flies

sometimes right out the window.

Golden rays blind me through the trees,

the sun cradled certain days each year

where the hills dip to a V,

though today it seems more wane

like it wears a dingy mourning veil,

tragic heroine of its own gothic tale.

Carol Edwards

The ghosts clinging here

never wish to leave

nor be by any other creature seen,

but their cobweb airs my ears still reach

whatever path I choose

dwelling long after each haunting strain

overshadows twilight's blues.

Spectrum in Blues

Roses are red, violets are blue

blue

blue like blues that wail

from a trumpet mouth,

pierces right through

the armor you built

to keep the longing out;

blue

blue and purple blues

that hit you and bruise

the cage keeping your heart compressed,

blues that shrill

from the reed clarinet

until the glass cracks—your crystal ball

where you sit

seeing all, feeling small—

spider web crawls letting the light through;

tears spill on blue

blue tears

on blue jeans, and green shoes

you bought because the color soothes,

edges tinged brown from use:

the lonely walks and silly jaunts

and blues dancing on a color sea

held so close to match rhythms, heartbeats;

blue

blue of the sky you never see anymore

never look up, only down

dark paths,

dark blues, harsh blues

like a saxophone crooning sweet nothings,

then nothing sweet

and the beat, beat

of pain, of fear—

purple, green, yellow

blooms

on dark skin, light skin

deeper than skin into red

that pumps in time to wailing

piercing

bruising

crooning

blues.

Carol Edwards

"From moonstone crushed"

From moonstone crushed, iridescent dust

adorns her skin, a lace overlay.

    Who knows the sorrows she hides within?

    Only the lonely moon, the gentle dawn,

    the wild ocean wind.

Carousel Horse

Harness cherry red, tassels golden shine
saddle dusky green, hooves bold as sky—

tinny notes chime into the cracks
gaping your porcelain back

innards empty but for the post
stabbed through, tarnished with age.

Your smooth nose and face belie
how many times
small child hands held too tight

winding the unvarying tune
sad minor keys trapped in endless parade.

Seeing you again, my heart
splits a little more

my hands bigger now
tender, but dumb
unable to glue you back together
any better than before.

Carol Edwards

Depth

for Ashlee

Somehow I can't write the words

the right way or the right order

to convey the depth of sadness

I feel over losing you to Death.

The waves of the sea are ever

changing, but there's always

the one that yanks you under

crushes you flat, like an avalanche.

The heaviness of water is forgotten

except by those most often

immersed in it, its power enough

to terrify them their whole lives.

 The World Eats Love

Those buried in dirt or ash bury likewise

in memories and grief the people

who loved them most but not best,

regret a most effective thorn.

I can't think of you even now

being weighed down by anything

here you left behind, and if joy

is so easily found over there, stay.

Carol Edwards

Autumn Ruins

The neighbor's dog kept me

a little bit company

while I traipsed down my blonding green

backyard ravine

to visit my creek, my secret fort

the shallow pools of rocks and sand.

I forgot that tiny wild irises

grow back here

and wavy-leafed plants

nipped close by nomad deer,

though untouched is

the spikey-leafed milk thistle.

Black bedrock slabs I hopped

sport a lichen carpet;

the one I napped on with my cat

sports a tree.

If I were child-sized

I could crawl beneath the bony boughs.

The World Eats Love

Once a vast kingdom,

now a desolate vale,

my childhood haven, imagination,

slowly collapsed

with adulthood's neglect,

skulls of past plays hid in grass.

Carol Edwards

Last. Time

sakura petals fall

at five centimeters per second

pink-tinged snow

crossing a rainbow

bridge in the limpid stream

clouding debris

settled down to sleep

time flowing into rivers and seas,

unmelting flakes

cascade, drifts piled

along folded edges

lying so still

quickened sometimes

by the wind

on whose breath they lift

forgotten longings stolen,

 The World Eats Love

prism light sings

on frequencies

the sakura and streams

can hear

plaintive call

of tears falling

frozen like snow

suspended long enough

to paint the world below.

Carol Edwards

Reunion

The ocean is gentle today

benignly chasing children and dogs and gulls

trailing after me like a bride's train

sometimes tangling about my legs.

She seems so sad with haze

clinging to her blue, horizon obscured

by smoke signals from fires further north

the sea helpless to give aid.

She shows her age

in tarnished silver-brown

like a wizened grandma to a child

suddenly ancient, wrinkled and small.

It's been so long since I last reached her

felt her cold hands on my skin—

my feet draw me closer to curling surf,

seek to fail at playing tag

like a tiny child delighted in the catching

the joyful hugs and kisses

and wriggling her escape in giggles and shrieks

stumbles off again, ever looking back.

Tidal matron arms wrap around my knees

reacquainting us with our familiality;

a knot somewhere inside finally releases,

roots deeply drink,

my washed-out footprints

a melancholy song of how long I stayed away,

how long I'll stay away again,

her little desert-dwelling ocean girl.

Carol Edwards

Trains

I'm not sure why I like trains.

I don't collect models

I don't care about design or form.

I know the basics of how they work

Like any vehicle.

Lots of movies feature the old coal-fueled kind

But the story captured my attention

Not the train.

I walk from my building to my car

Parked near railroad tracks

Where a train passes daily, several times, both ways

Blocks traffic

Blares its horn, deafens nearby pedestrians

Shuttles cargo and people from there to here.

I'm not sure why I like trains.

I used to watch one go by our house

With Mom and Dad

Race across the carpet to burst outside

Stop at the wire fence to the vineyard next door

Only one, once a day, sometimes at night.

On sunny days we'd worm through the fence

Walk the tracks

Grass and wildflowers poking up

Between the metal rails

The wood slats pitted and grooved from rain.

But the train stopped at one point.

They mended the wire fence.

I grew up

Left

And now watch a dusty train barrel on sizzling

Singing tracks

My pumps pinching my toes.

Carol Edwards

In Memory

Somewhere in a lonely place

the sun shines on placid grass

and on a lake holding deep blue secrets

and on a chair that's forgotten me.

Somewhere in a silent square

sits a table with an empty glass

waiting to be filled with wine

so you can take a sip, and sigh.

In a town somewhere

a wide yellow flower watches

the rubbled street below, watches for him

for his shade of hair, his silhouette at the door.

A small bridge over a small canal

holds hope the next step is hers,

holds to its post, a good stone soldier

base shattered overnight.

 The World Eats Love

And somewhere in a broken home

a man plays the same song on his piano

the pieces of his dream tied by strings

each key a key to holding them together:

blue and yellow butterflies in harmonic murmuration

murmuring the melody of who we used to be.

Carol Edwards

Forgotten Dreams

phantom shapes

by starlings made

    murmur of wings

    steals whole fancies

undaunted by fog or rain

in wide swathes the skies devour

settle for a moment, then

erupt again

    vanish in the waning clouds

    the graying sunset

only figments left

of something vaguely real

but like all dreams

in a world gone mad

pass away to warmer climes

    the cold suddenly too close

    to leave a trace behind.

Grow Up

Tiny little world

pretty crystal bead

filled with butterflies

sunshine, bubbling streams

trees for climbing,

tiny little world

merely marble-sized

big enough for oceans

rainbows

for bright and rainy skies,

little realm sphered in glass

radiant innocence

oblivious

like other little worlds

happy to be free

though of "freedom"

unknowing—

until you came

picked it up

tiny little life

and in your grip

cracked it

smacked it around

inside the circle

of your game

shook and shattered

the things inside

until it no longer sufficed

your perfect toy's

beauty marred

scars across its face.

   The World Eats Love

You left it in the dark alone

and like heat to cold

colors to gray seeped

light blotted out

flowers' faces leeched

wishes and dreams

shattered razor shards

eating bloodied feet

song and laughter unheard anymore

save perhaps a witch's cackle

(such an adult sound)

bubbling like boiled tar

from the heart you shred apart.

Carol Edwards

Tiny little world

kilter-less on the ground

collects around

so many more

hope and joy leaking out,

their rainbows mingle

with unholy oil

iridescent smears

a dark allure

merely waiting for a match.

Groomed

Inspired by the poet's sketch, "untitled"

It started with a face

trying to get the mouth and eyes

exactly right,

but even two-dimensional

looked like pits and a volcano.

Abandon the features—

just the skull shape,

outline with no face,

anonymous,

imagination fill in the blanks.

Then the leg, the part she

hates; her calves and ankles

have no curve

to differentiate,

so skip it, space

can infer. Next, pointed toe

so dainty and sweet,

dancer's feet

fit for a glass slipper

(it's a flat lie—her shoes are boats).

Make the thunder thighs

a thing of beauty,

so tired of photo manipulation

insisting stick skinny

the only worthwhile thing.

Finally, the breast, lifted,

perky, as girls are taught

is right, feeling silicone

secrets cup and push, whisper

all other shapes unsightly.

A portrait of the artist

as she thought would inspire love:

faceless, curvaceous, naked

coy and willing,

virgin sex goddess, lust titillating.

After so many years, the artist

grieves for what she lost

believing being a doll

was worth the heavy cost—

"desire" not the same as "value."

Carol Edwards

Mountain

We want a love like in a movie,
with the sweeping music and views so grand
where fights end, forgetting
and forgiving easy
people rough but genuine.

Has our dream made us happy?
Or has it bred misery
left us half believing in everything
yet persuaded by nothing
the pieces offered insufficient,

a crumbling loaf
fragments of itself dropped
for us to follow
until there's nothing left.

Crumbs cannot fill us
but the gold aura on the Silver Screen
plays frosting, sticks the bits back together
original shape barely recognized
though brightly colored
and made of the sweetness we crave.

Her Version Isn't You

Inside my armored heart

the child I outgrew

still hangs her joy and hopes

on the pedestal she made you:

    imaginary friend

    beloved prince charming

seeing only the nicest colors,

and these she blends

until the pretend

is nothing like the owner.

Carol Edwards

Darkened Stage

Shadows dance

a midnight revelry

all concealed, transformed,

shaped to their own image

no longer play

their daylight rôle,

lying teeth and tongues

in darkness feast

surge of fangs and heat

between bodies—

> I cannot see you over me
>
> but I know that we are not
>
> who we met under the sun.

Bird of Prey

Betrayal's wet talons drip

ichor on the page

oily dark smear

where your heart lies open

beating

her razor beak

shredding to pieces

tendon by tendon

Love laid bare

living nightmare

Carol Edwards

her acid scream

sears through spine

bubbles skin

deforms whimpered cries

paralyzed

you lie, bound under

her merciless ministrations

simmering strings

defacing innocent loyalty

When the Monster Under Your Bed Has Become Your Friend

Inspired by Linda D. Addison's "How to Recognize a Demon Has Become Your Friend"

Another day done

another wasted chance

another wound, future scar

pinprick

or gash

skin bruise, heart bruise—it all blurs as one,

crawl battered into bed

the monster underneath

reaches for my hand.

He doesn't understand

why I tell him, "Wait. Wait. There's still

some good somewhere.

I can't give up yet."

Carol Edwards

Perhaps one day

as monsters do

he'll watch you stir another ruse

and disregard the words I said;

instead

in darkness as you sleep

he'll creep his coils around your feet

python slow, until

he's swallowed you in his grip,

jointed spindle legs

your chest will rip

his aim to hold in taloned hand

your heart, still beating.

Into it he'll sink his fangs, a ripened plum,

your blood the nectar he desires,

eyes aglow with molten fires.

Your throat he'd crush

with a single blow:

silent your screams as he

devours your eyes,

such delicacies.

Patiently so far he bides

sensing the slow sap of hope I hold.

Once it's gone

and under the bed I crawl

safer there than prison walls,

through my hair his claws will run

until I sleep,

and then your time has come.

Carol Edwards

To My Sweet Flower

Ash butterflies flit above

Dancing blooms with sharp tongues

Bright they flutter, wings lined

In glowing sunset red,

I am a different monster now

Wildfire rage tamed

To sleeping volcano

Heating the ground under your feet

Heaving in currents thick and deep,

I like my fangs

So new and sharp

Hungry for *the* kill

Not just any

Messy blood smears in my wake,

On you I'll feed most assuredly

A little at a time

Each minute stoking your desire

Until my poison seeps into your veins

And I unearth to tangle you

In my igneous sheets.

Carol Edwards

Petals

from our mouths

scatter

shine in candlelight

      smooth edges

      whetted sharp

crack and shatter

under us

glittering shards

      burrow in our eyes

      beneath our skin

bloodthirsty slivers

slice

through veins

      cruel fangs

      crave a feast.

The World Eats Love

                    Wet shadows

                        hide

             petals curled dry

            crumbled

        lifeless

                     rotted scent

                         blent

                 with rust stains.

Carol Edwards

The Love Vine

The love vine said to the young oak,

"You are beautiful, I love you."

The young oak believed it, let it grow

up her base and trunk.

Their leaves grew beautiful and green,

flowers and fruit full.

The love vine kept whispering,

"You're beautiful, I love you."

The oak believed it, even when its stinging

roots burrowed under her skin,

into her arms and fingers.

"You're beautiful, I love you."

The vine's flowers and fruit grew.

The oak tree barely changed. In drought

she turned brittle. The vine's leaves stayed green.

"No one loves you like I do."

"I love you, you're beautiful."

The oak reached to sky, to sun.

In summer, she waited for cool nights;

in winter, she waited for rain.

Her roots drew in as much as she could hold.

The vine's leaves and flowers and fruit grew.

The oak stood, arms reaching, the vine woven thickly.

"I'm the only one who can love you."

The old oak stooped, arms crumbled,

fingers snapped. Her roots drank no water.

The vine whispered, "How could you betray me,

I loved you." The oak regretted every second

it ever touched her. In autumn,

the old oak waited for the lightning, the fire, the wind.

Carol Edwards

History

Roots bury deep

reaching for voiceless things

    unable to leave

    the dead

    where they lie,

In darkness

ends twine through skulls' eyes

    bones of old loves

    suffocated hopes

    buried alive,

Monarchs of their fertile kingdoms

greener for the refuse

hidden under stems

    where deepest secrets

    tightest cling,

Writhing dance

puppeted by memory strings

fuels their frenzies

    feasting on decay

    in wild revelry.

Did it Hurt When You Fell?

The moon shuts her eye
weeping for Light sacrificed—
her tears burn to Earth.

Vacant from the ground my eyes stare.
I cannot move, cannot close them;
the wind steals my tears
robs my tongue.

Night falls as I lie here
lips cracked, peeling
hips twisted
one foot wrenched and strung.

I feel a spider creep delicately
across my cheek;
the night's cold seizes heat
turns my blood to viscous honey.
Even the moon looks away
hides her face in blackest sheets.

Carol Edwards

The owl and the raven
converse together how best
to peck out my soft parts
before the coyotes claim their pound of flesh
and the insects burrow through to bone.

You told me love was heaven, and I an angel
in it; you're hardly God, yet here I am
cast down—the fate of all who believe you—
corpses piled high enough to be
a second Babel tower

monument to all the lies you spill.
Water and blood ribbons
trickle over torn limbs
insatiable the mouths beneath them

tattered wings plucked naked
fodder for silk divans, satin pillows
perhaps woven on the lace
adorning your latest angel
soon cast down to your floor.

The World Eats Love

Something Sweet

Kisses dissolve on my tongue

like caramel and marshmallow;

bitterness follows.

I've lost my taste for you.

Carol Edwards

My Love

It's cold here

the icy air before snow

seeps in under skin and clothes

the killing kind, without the glitter or shine

of pristine white beauty blinding in the sunlight.

This is meant to freeze, to still and atrophy

to sink to bones and never leave

blacken careless naked ends

creep along blood bends

crystals in its wake…

til heartbeats

cease.

Last. Step

It was just enough

the air pressed out of your lungs

      punctured balloons

      flattened

the hole so small

I had to stand there and push

      molehill under a mountain

the weight snapping

bone bars

      cage for a wild thing

      fluttering clipped wings,

I called it a mercy

to crush you out of your misery

and you see nothing

but black, and ash

the world burning,

Though that could be a trick

of your eyes' light

finally dying

its soul to join others of its kind

in the reaching sunrise

touching color

back into life

its fingertips, like mine

bloodstained

Things Are Louder When It's Cold

I open my window to feel the wind,
to hear the frogs' singing.
Winter still clings to the metal frame;
so far the frogs are silent.

The cold twines around my fingers and hair,
cold like the hands you used to grab
me, pull me to you like a whore,
cold your grin and your eyes.

The lid cannot open when a jar sits on
the windowsill all night, metal and glass crystalized.
She tips over the ledge, gets lost in tall grass.
In the morning, the sun finds her shining pieces.

The wind understands carrying melodies on the cold,
just as the frogs understand winter's ending.
Your fingers find biting teeth coiled in sunlight.
For me, the frogs start singing.

Carol Edwards

The Fall

Living rib formed into a frame
echo of the Song long singing,

    dove and dahlia
    butterfly and rose

        rooted splendor longs to fly—

wings lift up her eyes
to highest cirrus down

    warmth of sun
    on every pinion,
    freedom's glory
    alight on every scale;

but you, in malicious waste
loosed the barb
to pierce lung, heart

unsightly vermin your eye abhorred

to ground scored

and deeper in, wrapped by thorns

the rose and dahlia

blinded

                                                                                                 die

severed from bluest bright paradise

in fetid darkness condemned to lie;

breathing cage overrun

gasps her last

collapses

flesh withered to unfeeling stone

and to dust return her bones.

Carol Edwards

Avalanche

If the tears we cried left tracks

and the lies against us scars,

mountains were made of all of us

carved faces pale as stars,

If betrayals left broken bones

and hatreds dark bruises bloomed,

the entire world lay one mass grave

returning silver to the moon,

If kindness healed torn up pieces

and loving words restored—

too late. Avalanches crush their breath

their blood the seas engorge

Normalize

A synonym for believe is trust

and broken trust is par for the course nowadays—

doesn't make the injustice any less:

person on a soapbox bares wide the sins

of a conglomerate, figure, nation

decries some unspeakable the rest of us

simply think, "You should have expected it,"

before passing by, calloused walled

hearts brush off the raw betrayal

in their eyes, their face, because we've

already been there, banged our fists and heads

relentless against metal doors until we bled,

and over time accepted apathy as normalcy,

picked ourselves back up,

wondered why we were so angry.

This is simply how it is.

Carol Edwards

Last. Breath

folded together

petals

on a dying rose

softness turned brittle

crumbles

at a touch

bud broken open

secrets poured out

kiss-and-tell scent

draws hungry lovers

to mount and burrow

eat their fill,

 The World Eats Love

bared naked

to the merciless sun

rot begins

veined heart

adrift

unhinged—

loving earth

at last enfolds

Carol Edwards

I'm the Lungs Now

"Tell you what,"

I say to myself,

"you finish this email

and as reward you can go make

your baked potato—

it'll be done about 5

and you'll be hungry by then."

But I'm hungry now.

Not just in my belly, that'll keep

for an hour;

hungry under my skin,

in the dark somewhere

I never let people in, not really.

Hungry for LIFE,

hungry for the love and the soul

of someone who will feed me willingly

after seeing the dark,

 The World Eats Love

their love for me a power I use to keep

them here,

my love for them

what tethers, brings them back again,

like I used to do for ones

hungry for me

but not for *me*—just what I'd give

to keep their attention, so easily withdrawn

so easily thrown away

when that was all I had to keep breathing.

Now I'm hungry

but not like them:

give <u>me</u> your love and soul to eat—

the real stuff

none of this cotton candy fluff—

and to you I'll give air

so you can breathe,

finally.

Carol Edwards

Apparition

My eyes see nothing but a wall,

a floor, and an empty wooden chair—

but my heart sees you

haunting all the space

until transformed it becomes

a play of twilight rendezvous

in that place I'm free to love you.

Unseen, you follow me,

through walls and doors you move

trailing down aisles and streets

your voice a hum

blending with the crowd

lost in a labyrinth

of dreams and fantasies

that twine together

thorny rose vines

holding sweetness in the air I breathe

yet prick my fingers when I reach.

The World Eats Love

Am I allowed to speak my love?

this poor thing barely living—

its bouts of ecstasy and fear

that maim and murder daily

then resurrect each morning

and burrow into you

canker in your bud

devour and possess you

bloody evidence of hunger left

in that place I'm free to love you.

Carol Edwards

Forbidden

You were so thin

in my dream

like you were wasting away,

I felt the press of your bones

when you crawled into my arms

lay on top of me,

you weren't like this before.

I held you close

half afraid I'd break you

angered at the words

and thoughts people used

to chip away your soul,

prying eyes hurling

acid barbs, poison darts;

   The World Eats Love

I felt you wither more.

Their words tore us—

you stood, left

almost nothing, shadowless.

I roamed mountains and seascapes

to a dark place

lay down alone

to dream or to die

I didn't know,

but like a ghost

you walked through the wall

waited for my arms to reach for you

embrace you

light as a feather, gray as breath,

no bones to feel anymore

the phantom, or dream, of you

blended with shadows

forbidden kisses we never succumbed to

held in our mouths

at last to drink.

Shallow Grave

A breath catches in my chest

as the wind's fingers

brush my collar bone.

I would the wind were your breath,

and its fingers, yours

to caress the ribs beneath

and free what's caged

into your hands,

unhinge its thin covering.

    Rain falls and lingers where it will—

    your love the downpour

    to sate my desert thirst.

Carol Edwards

Deep Water

Two sea lions meet in deep water.
Their sleek heads surface, shadows
on silver. Ripples carry moonlight
to a hidden shore. The lions float close
together, dive back under, bodies curved.

You lie on sand next to me. I trace
the black swirls in your skin, signs
of tribe, of life, of family. Moonlight
makes me pale, but it streams off you
like water, hugs your lines as it falls.

The lions dance under the water's
curl, send ruffles to our feet.
I follow the lines of you, cup the
moonlight and drink. In the dark I see
your smile, your eyes, the places
your fingers stray, valleys on the moon.

The lions' ballet echoes on land:

with sweet words you immerse me,

with touches of your strong hands.

Your voice bewitches my existence.

Your kiss weaves a madness

into my bones.

And I breathe in deep water.

Carol Edwards

Shell Lining

Rainbow auroras wrapped in midnight

fade

like the sky prism after rain

like the memories of the day

I found them,

found you;

Rewashed with water

the colors return

but never the same

as when I pulled them from the waves,

full of their native salt and sand;

From their wet land

I carried them to mine

where thirsty light

devours fog and mist,

magic drops forever lost;

So quick to desiccate

evaporate

only a pale silver sheen remains

teases at what was

what might have been,

had I stayed when you asked me to.

Carol Edwards

Midnight Oasis

The summer sunset layers red and gold.

A drop of sweat follows your spine
        like my finger did that time
        when we lay naked to the wind

sultry and warm, moon full
        and the Night Queen bloomed
        brightest goddess in the garden.

She closed forever in the morning.

Our hearts ache as we gaze
        at the roads we took
        another age to wait,

sun burning tender ends
        of fragile ivy leaves
        that cling to crumbling lattices.

Waiting

I.

Wings dance along the light strand,

their shadows playing dapple games.

A hot wind sways cottonwood leaves,

rustle of paper chimes.

She stands by the thin stream,

summer silver ribbon

in waning moonlight,

her dress white

gaze fixed on the stars

waiting

for her love who returned there,

breathless promises a thunder

only she can hear—

night's deepest black

trapped in his eyes,

skin of fire

soft as velvet rain

breathing through the trellis frame

its whisper his voice

gliding on the storm,

wings to lift her free

of crushing reality.

II.

Sparks dance along wiring exposed,

char marks playing dapple games.

Hot air swells like currents deep

rising to overflow.

He lies by a streak of blood,

his own,

smeared waterfall

pools on the deck below

breaths held between his lungs

waiting

for the memories of her

to veil his eyes,

her face all he sees—

eyes bright as nebula light

deep as his homeland's sea,

skin thin as flowers' breath

soft as desert winds

that warm on moonless nights,

her voice the song of space,

kisses whispered lightning strikes,

their fire almost enough

to defy the stars his fate.

Moths

From light to light I skip,

each a glowing moon

      gently they light the path.

Her feet trip in wooden shoes

as she follows to find you.

      Will we find what we seek

      at the lonely trail's end?

Our loves drift in Heaven's

River—we have no boat

or bridge to reach,

      only our hearts on wings

      fluttering restless.

Carol Edwards

Snowbound

A boy sits on a train
snowbound
in the middle of nowhere
storm layering
frozen hopes
over the tracks,

A girl waits on a bench
frozen
in the middle of nowhere
hope layered
with delicate sculptures
crushed under her feet,

Pristine wilderness rages—
frozen tears
join biting flakes
abducted by wind
blood slowly stilled,

    searching lanterns silenced

Windows

I'd rather live in poetry lines

    than this world of bills and broken dreams—

        Poets' words

            trapped together on pages

                looking-glass windows:

                    Poets' souls

              genies in lamps

            worlds in wardrobes:

        open the spine

    the dream re-find

Love and sight regain:

        see reality

            see the Really-real

                set inside dark lines

the place our spirits hide to nourish back alive.

Carol Edwards

I grieve this place of heartbreak

    of long-inflicted pain

        "Real" life:

            feelings, beliefs, lies

                so easily spoon-fed:

                    wet shadows

                stuck in window corners

            smeared by fingers burrowed

    in open wounds

  slick mucous coated:

flies eyeing

the place our spirits slowly die, God reduced to synapses firing.

The Really-real shows the Real

    differently:

        razor edges sting the Song of longing

            Love in every windowpane

                pain

            a window for Love

    to strip the façade "Real" made her wear

        ill-fitted and grotesque

to sing outside the boundary, unblind eyes seeking.

Star-Song

calls to dust inside us

we don't belong here

encased by water and skin and fear

        force of gravity

        binds our bodies

we all carry

kernels of singularity

        filled with yearning

        for our Origin

calling

to shed our prisons

        in soul-fire drown

glittering strands

unraveling

        for Love to weave

        between eternities

Carol Edwards

Whisper-Steps of the Really-Real

All things end.

It's all we know

      a beginning to end to beginning…

      even "continue"

is collected ends

      neat in a row.

The Really-real

      echoes

      in transports of Love, of awe

            heaviness released

            heart-flight

                  ever-light ballet step…

Ends. Gravity

      lead heavy guardian

      of the merely Real

            taking, talking, mocking

                scrashing glass

                    blindness.

The Really-real
>   stirs heart strings with longing
>   tender heart-tears
>   feelings
>   ever-light
>   breathing…

Ends. Drowned
>   by oceans of merely Real
>   no-feel
>   no-where
>   no-breath
>   light sucked out
>   crushing emptiness…

Endless.

The Really-real speaks
>   across the nothing,
>   one Word left…

>   "Come!"

Carol Edwards

Across Dark Waters

Death takes me to meet the One I love,

her cold hand a relief from the heat of living,

the mountain winds lift

white petals to glittering skies.

I wait on the banks of Heaven's River—

the sun has fallen, the flood rushes dark.

I hear my Love's voice over the water,

my veil sweeps away as I cross.

Dawn rises as I behold my Love—

strong currents cannot drown my sight.

Found

A windchime's soprano
sings a single note

space-time sprints
along a sunray

morning's first
unzips a gateway—

the Really-real waits
just past the waves

ocean of light
thunderous, blinding
crests and curls
over my feet

cool wind warms souls
dries tears

and Love rushes in
longing embraced

pain melted away:
"At last, I've found you."

Carol Edwards

 The World Eats Love

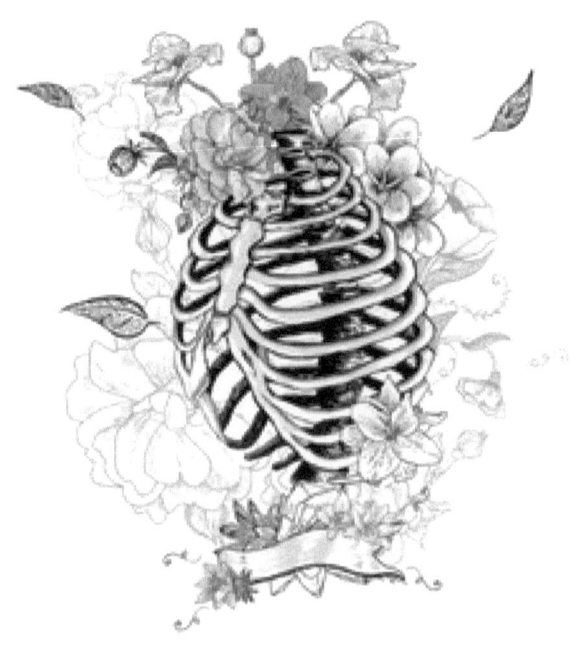

Carol Edwards

The Lonely Shoes

A Short Story

Once upon a time, inside a shoe factory in no place in particular, a pair of shoes emerged from the depths of machinery. A woman standing by the assembly line saw them and said, "Oh, what a pretty pair of shoes!" The shoes liked this and glowed for her.

Another woman further down also saw them, and said, "How pretty! I do love red." She carefully closed the lid of the shoes' box, whispering to them, "I hope you find a good home and that your wearer will love you."

The shoes smiled to themselves. *Why, yes. We* are *pretty. We will be loved by everyone. We will be purchased the first day people see us.*

The day came when a shopkeeper proudly opened the shoes' box and put them on display in his store. "These are very nice shoes," he said. "I will sell many of these."

The shoes sat smugly on the shelf near the center of the store. *We are the prettiest shoes here,* they thought. *Those other shoes are so bland, black and brown and tan. No one will want those shoes when they see us.*

The first customer walked in. "How delightful! A pair of red shoes! I wonder if they fit." She took one off the shelf and put it on. "They're a little tight." She took the other off the shelf and put it on. "No, these shoes are too small. Perhaps the shopkeeper has more."

The woman took off the shoes and set them back on the shelf. The shoes felt disappointed, but one cannot expect to fit every foot. *Someone with the right-sized feet will find u*s, they thought.

We will be purchased and worn and loved always.

Another customer walked in. "Oh my, how daring, red shoes! They look my size. Just trying them on won't hurt..." She took both shoes off the shelf and tried them on, but they kept slipping off her heel. "Oh dear," the woman said, "These are too big, even though the tag says my size." She took them off and put them back. "I'll just get a normal pair of black shoes. Black goes with everything." The woman moved away down the aisle, a disappointed expression on her face.

The shoes felt equally disappointed. *That's okay,* they thought. *Not everyone with this size foot has the same width or length. There will be someone else, surely.*

Days passed, and many people tried on the pair of pretty red shoes, but always with the same result: too small, too big, not wide enough, not tall enough, not low enough—somehow not quite right. The shoes started to feel stretched and worn and tired. And sad. *Is there something wrong with us?* they wondered. *All these other shoes are being purchased. Were we made wrong?*

Many more days passed, and people stopped trying on the pretty red shoes. A few customers here and there would glance at them, and maybe one would say, "Oh. Red shoes."

One day, the shopkeeper took the shoes off his display shelf and put them back in their box. "You're the last ones," he said to them, "and nobody seems interested."

The shoes lay limply in the tissue paper. *It's not our fault,* they thought. *We really thought someone would want us.*

The shopkeeper slapped a sticker on the side of the box and put the shoes under a red sign at the back of the store.

The shoes lay in the box for many weeks, consoling themselves, thinking, *Just because we're at the back of the store doesn't mean we won't have a home. We're still pretty, and so many people like red. Red means exciting and fun. We're fun, right?*

Customers came and went from the rack at the back of the store. Sure, several people tried on the shoes, but never with any admiration or praise. They simply analyzed according to price and fit, then moved on.

One afternoon, the shopkeeper put another sticker on the side of the box, but the shoes couldn't see what it said.

The next day, the shoes lay all day in their box, untouched, almost unnoticed. The chime of the door's bell periodically punctuated the din of ambient music and scattered conversations. The shoes listened, despondent. They could hear the shopkeeper's voice weave through the various sounds of excited shoppers, energetic children, shoes being tried on, taken off, boxes shuffled in their stacks.

But then the shopkeeper's voice seemed to get louder. "…with me." He walked into the back section with someone wearing scuffed brown loafers under starting-to-fray gray slacks. "Back here is where we keep shoes that were on the shelf for too long or were replaced by a newer style."

The feet shuffled nervously. "I just want to be able to give my wife a birthday present she'll enjoy, and I know she loves shoes. I wrote down her size, but I'm a bit out of my depth here."

"I understand completely, sir."

"My wife has expensive taste," the man continued, "but

things have been… difficult lately. I was hoping you had something…" He left the sentence unfinished.

The shopkeeper knelt and pulled the red shoes' box off the bottom. "I believe these are the size you need." He handed the box to the man—tall, with a dark blue tie and white shirt. "Would these be the sort of thing you're looking for?"

The tall man stared in awe at the shoes. "They're lovely," he said. "They're exactly what I think she'll like. Thank you so much!"

Finally! thought the shoes joyously. *We will have a home! We will be loved!*

The shopkeeper closed the shoes inside their box, and at the man's request, wrapped them in the pretty silver paper they'd seen him use with so many other shoe boxes. The shoes shifted awkwardly as they felt the tall man tuck the package under his arm, and again when they heard him opened a whisper-squeaky door, his breathing the only other sound.

After what seemed like an eternity, the shoes heard the murmur of sleepy voices, the swish of feet on carpet, and suddenly the door clicked opened. A shriek of delight followed. "Honey," a woman cried, "you didn't forget!"

"Of course not, my love." The man sounded pleased. "Open them. I think you'll like them."

The shoes waited impatiently as the wife tore the wrapping paper off their box. *Almost,* they thought. *Almost…*

The wife yanked the lid off the box, pulled back the tissue paper, then stopped. She just looked at them and said nothing.

"Darling? Are you alright," the man asked, suddenly

sounding anxious. He sat on the end of a bed, paused in tying a gray bathrobe around his waist.

"They're red," she said. "I never wear red."

"But… you said the other day you wanted a brighter pair, that you have so many dark ones –."

"I meant white or pastel, not RED." The wife tossed the box on the floor, the shoes smacking together like a slap. "You're going to take them back."

The man winced. "There was a no refunds or exchanges sticker on the box," he replied quietly. "I thought you'd really like them…"

"Based on what?" she snarled. "These are nothing like what I wear. Nothing. I wouldn't be caught dead in them."

The man's face turned a shade lighter, and for a second his eyes wavered. "I had other plans for today, my love," he started slowly, "brunch at your favorite club, with mimosas, and shopping with Sedhu and Gabby…"

The woman's face smoothed, and she smiled. "On The Boulevard?"

The man nodded as he stood. "Of course, darling. Anything for you." His shoulders hunched a little as he walked out, like a weight resettled.

After a moment of silence, the woman addressed the closet, glaring at the shoes. "I'll deal with YOU later," she hissed. "Stupid, garish, last-season pumps."

The shoes lay in despair on the floor of the closet. *We're ugly,*

they thought. *We're outdated. No one will love us.*

After a few hours, a different woman appeared, wearing a bland uniform. She picked up the open box without so much as a second glance. "Off to the donation center for you," she muttered.

The shoes tried to stop caring. They tried not to notice being lumped in a bin with dirty work boots and torn flip flops. They tried not to think of their days in the fancy shop as they were shoved unceremoniously on a metal shelf next to grubby sneakers. They tried not to feel lonely when other shoes were grabbed and thrown into baskets and taken home.

The shoes stopped paying attention to anything. Their toes rubbed with dust and their edges flagged. Kids played with them, tromped in them, tossed them under the shelves so exhausted employees had to fish them out and put them back. *Surely,* they thought, *surely, we will leave even here, unwanted, and end up in a landfill.*

But then, one evening, all the shoes perked up. A gentle step paced slowly down the aisle.

It's her, all the shoes thought to each other. *It's her. Someone who still cares about us.*

There had been other shoppers that excited items in the store. They didn't act like other customers. They handled things carefully, like they still had value. They would admire the pieces they picked up, and every so often, put an item in their basket.

The red shoes lay on their sides, unconcerned with the ripple of anticipation in their section. They didn't want to get their hopes up, didn't want to be poked, prodded, examined, and rejected yet again. *No more,* they thought. *Just go away.*

But a shadow fell across them, lingering. "Oh," a voice exclaimed quietly. "It can't be."

The shoes became curious. They listened.

"I wanted these shoes, but I couldn't afford them." The woman picked them carefully off their perch, brushed off the dust and dirt. "They still look so beautiful."

The red shoes perked up a little. *We're beautiful?*

The woman took off her brown sandals. "I hope they fit."

We hope we fit, thought the shoes.

She slipped on one pump. "They feel so soft."

The shoes beamed.

She slipped on the other. "I have such a hard time finding my size just right." The shoes practically glowed as the woman turned and twirled in front of a mirror. "They're perfect," she breathed, eyes shining.

We're perfect, thought the shoes.

The woman took them off and held them to her chest. "I've been looking for you for so long. You'll come home with me now, and I'll wear you, and love you always."

And they lived happily ever after.

 The World Eats Love

Carol Edwards

Acknowledgements

I offer sincere gratitude to my editors, E. Mery Blake and Kara Hawkers, whose enthusiasm and encouragement led to the conception and development of this collection. Thank you for enduring my endless questions with patience and grace.

Deepest thanks to SFPA Grand Master Linda D. Addison, the first editor to accept a poem of mine for publication, who has been a constant source of encouragement, wisdom, inspiration, and light in my poetry journey.

I wish to gush All The Magnificent Things over Lisa Walsh for being my sole Safe Reader, for always expressing delight to read my poems, and gifting me with kind, joyous words.

May Mountains Of Blessings grace Cody Knocke and Deanna Cross, my beta readers, whose feedback helped reveal this collection's bigger picture.

A huge thank you to Sharon Skinner—writer, poet, and freelance editor/book coach—for giving me invaluable critique on "The Lonely Shoes" nearly a decade ago, which allowed it to grow into the story it is now.

An Amazonian bear hug to my family—Mom, Dad, Mary Anne, and Mike—and to the countless friends across different stages of my life, and to my faithful followers on social media, for their spontaneous support, prayers, and celebrations for the many milestones in this adventure. Your uplifting comments, direct messages, and hugs mean so much.

Finally, I cannot fail to acknowledge the relentless editor in my head, the one who taught me all the rules of proper grammar and punctuation—that I then ignore in this collection—my junior high English teacher, Sandra Peters.

I gratefully acknowledge the following publications (and their editors) wherein these poems first appeared, sometimes in slightly different form:

Cajun Mutt Press, 2021
"Trains"

the leaves fall, 2021
"Autumn Ruins"

Otherwise Engaged Literary and Art Journal: Volume 8, 2021
"Instructions to Break Your Own Heart"
"Daydreams"
"Haunted"
"Something Sweet"

Trouvaille Review, 2021
"Reunion"

Panoply, 2022
"Peeling a Tangelo"

POETiCA REViEW, Issue 13, 2022
"Depth"

#AERATION, 2022
"Avalanche"

Where Flowers Bloom, 2022
"In Memory"

Balm 2, 2022
"Our Hungers"
"Last. Words"
"I'm the Lungs Now"
"Tattoo"
"Old Sweatshirt"
"When the Monster Under Your Bed Has Become Your Friend"

The Post Grad Journal, Issue 5, 2023
"Things are Louder When It's Cold"

Carol Edwards

About the Author

CAROL EDWARDS is a northern California native transplanted to southern Arizona. She lives and works in relative seclusion with her books, plants, and pets (2 dogs, 5 cats, + husband). She grew up reading fantasy and classic novels, climbing trees, and acquiring frequent grass stains. She currently enjoys a coffee addiction and raising her succulent army.

Her poetry has appeared in numerous publications, including *Space & Time*, *OpenDoor Magazine*, *Uproar Literary Blog* by The Lawrence House Centre for the Arts, *Heart of Flesh Literary Journal*, *Cajun Mutt Press*, *Gyroscope Review*, *Agape Review*, *Open Skies Quarterly*, *Trouvaille Review*, *Otherwise Engaged Literary and Art Journal*, *MockingOwl Roost*, *POETiCA REViEW*, *Panoply*, *The Sunshine Press*, and *The Post Grad Journal*.

She published a mini-chap with Origami Poems Project titled *Where You'll Find Me*.

Her poetry has also appeared in several anthologies: *the ocean waves*, *the leaves fall*, *Words for the Earth*, and *Where Flowers Bloom* from Red Penguin Books; *Balm 2*, *Cherish*, *Tempest*, and *Evermore 2* from The Ravens Quoth Press; *The Moon and Stars in the Evening Sky*, *Dragonflies and Fairies*, *The Wonders of Winter*, and *Love Letters in Poetic Verse* from Southern Arizona Press; *#AERATION*, and *#GROUNDINGEARTH* from White Stag Publishing.

Two of her poems are scheduled for inclusion in *#SPIRIT*, an anthology from White Stag Publishing, to be released October 2023.

Another of her poems is scheduled for inclusion in *UNDER HER EYE*, an anthology from Black Spot Books, to be released November 2023.

She is a member of the Science Fiction & Fantasy Poetry Association (SFPA).

Follow her on Instagram, Twitter, and Facebook. She also sporadically uploads her poetry to her website: practicallypoetical.wordpress.com.

Instagram @practicallypoetical
Twitter @practicallypoet
Facebook @practicallypoet

 The World Eats Love

Carol Edwards

About the Publisher

THE RAVENS QUOTH PRESS is a boutique publisher based in Australia, dedicated to showcasing the best of international poetry craft in beautifully presented publications.

Follow us: **linktr.ee/TheRavensQuothPress**

Carol Edwards

The World Eats Love

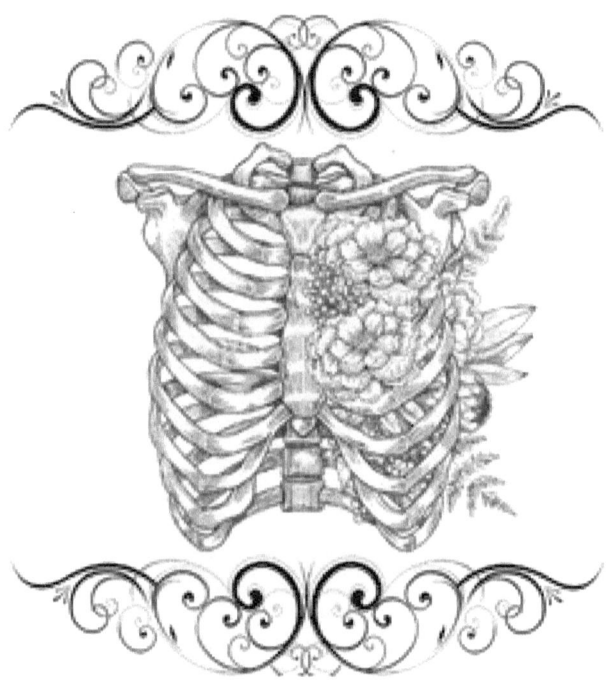

www.ingramcontent.com/pod-product-compliance
Lightning Source LLC
Chambersburg PA
CBHW020325010526
44107CB00054B/1980